T0156942

# So You Want
## *to be*
# Married

*A Godly Foundation for Marriage*

### Lady M
(and contributing authors)

iUniverse, Inc.
New York   Bloomington

**So You Want to Be Married**
**A Godly Foundation for Marriage**

*iUniverse books may be ordered through booksellers or by contacting:*

*iUniverse*
*1663 Liberty Drive*
*Bloomington, IN 47403*
*www.iuniverse.com*
*1-800-Authors (1-800-288-4677)*

*Because of the dynamic nature of the Internet, any Web addresses or links contained in this book may have changed since publication and may no longer be valid. The views expressed in this work are solely those of the author and do not necessarily reflect the views of the publisher, and the publisher hereby disclaims any responsibility for them.*

*ISBN: 978-1-4502-5062-7 (sc)*
*ISBN: 978-1-4502-5064-1 (ebook)*

*Printed in the United States of America*

*iUniverse rev. date: 09/27/2010*

# Dedication

To my beautiful mother and my precious children.

# Acknowledgement

This book would not have been birthed if not for my Lord and Savior, so all praises and honor are due to Him. I would like to express my deepest gratitude for the prayers and support of my family, my presiding Bishop Paul and Co-Pastor Debra Morton, and friends. I'm truly honored.

Words cannot express my sincere thanks to the contributing authors, who have plowed the field to make this book become reality. Much agape to Prophetess Pamela Whatley, Ministers Jerome and Rhonda Thomas, Minister Kevin Lewis, Author Yolanda Marshall, Pastor Hakeem J. Webb, Financial Advisor Zenobia Mims, Deacon Anthony, and Sister Denise Reed. These vessels of God spoke life into this book and took time to write some of the chapters and prayers.

Thank you, my sisters and brothers in the body of Christ, for writing your testimony regarding being married, single, or divorced to minister to the hearts of the people.

# CONTENTS

## Preparing For Marriage

# Introduction

This book is a guide to dating and marriage. It will walk you through key steps to having a successful marriage in the Lord. It teaches the keys to embrace your singleness with the Lord and the patience to wait for the man or woman of "valor." This book is a testimony from circumstances I have dealt with regarding my own relationships that were not in alignment with God's purpose and plan, but initiated by my own will, even years later after entering into a marriage that ended in divorce. A year ago, during my separation, the Lord pressed upon my heart the inspiration to write this book to express the importance of seeking God in your friendship, courtship, and marriage.

The Lord spoke His word to me in the summer of 2009 to write this book for the women and men who desire to be married, but only think about the hype of the wedding day and forget about the vows, the commitment, and the true meaning of marriage.

During this time of my development, I asked God to provide me with the areas of the book that would minister to the heart of His people so they may receive the knowledge to wait for that special mate chosen by our Father.

Throughout the book, there are testimonies from fellow brothers and sisters of the body that share words of encouragement. Various contributing authors share their knowledge, experience, and expertise in the areas of brokenness, premarital counseling, preparing you to become the husband/ wife pleasing to God, and finances.

# About the Author

**Lady M**

Lady M is a licensed and ordained minister of the gospel who facilitates group discussion forums about relationships for single women. She has always had an eye for creating fabulous affairs, and opened her first event planning business at the age of 19. She is the Coordinating Producer of a Wedding Network, an online and television network in Atlanta, Georgia; and has been the host of several radio, online, and television shows. She is also CEO of Destined Enterprises, the umbrella company of Creative Occasions Event Planning, an outreach ministry facilitating seminars and conferences for women, publications for online magazine and books, and cosmetic products. She is currently pursuing a degree in Christian Ministries and plans to obtain degrees in Counseling and a Ph.D. in Divinity. She plans to teach at a college and continue her ministry to help women succeed in relationships. A native of Connecticut, Lady M currently resides in Atlanta with her two children.

# Contributing Authors

## Yolanda Marshall

Author/Evangelist Yolanda Marshall is a native of Birmingham, Alabama, currently residing in Lithia Springs, Georgia. She holds a bachelor's degree in Business Administration from Faulkner University in Montgomery, Alabama, and a master's degree in Management from Troy University in Montgomery, Alabama. Yolanda is the author of *From Victim to Virtuous*, a self-help book for broken girls and women to help them heal from the pain of dealing with unhealthy relationships, dating a married man, speaking word curses into relationships. She is also the owner of Lady of Virtue Gifts and Apparel, an online business offering Christian T-shirts for women, men, and children.

## Ministers Jerome and Rhonda Thomas

The founders and CEO'S of United for Life, Marriage and Family Ministry, Ft. Lauderdale, Florida. Jerome and Rhonda have been married for over 24 years and believe in the sanctity and unity of marriage. Their ministry was birthed from adversities and trials they suffered as a result of not receiving Godly counseling. Their testimonials and teachings of victory, reconciliation, unity, strength, and restoration radically transform and restore lives. Their goal is to guide couples, singles, and families to reach their destiny through the Word of God.

## Minister Kevin Lewis, Ph.D.

Kevin Lewis was born and raised in Atlanta, Georgia, by a loving family that instilled in him sound Biblical principles that continue to govern his life. Kevin received double bachelor's degrees from the University of Virginia and a master's degree in Counseling from Argosy University. He was conferred a Doctorate of Divinity from Emanuel Theological Seminary. Kevin is an ordained minister, retired from the Atlanta Police Department, where he served as Director of Chaplains for fifteen years. Kevin's passion remains in the area of ministry and counseling, both pastoral and clinical, assisting individuals and families in achieving a higher quality of life. Kevin is the author of *Brothers Together* and co-author of *Lessons Learned That Anchored Souls and Daily Dose Inspirations.*

## Financial Advisor Zenobia D. Mims

Zenobia D. Mims is a licensed Independent Representative with Primerica Financial Services, the largest marketing services company in North America. She is licensed in Georgia and in her home state of Louisiana. Zenobia is passionate about helping families reach their financial goals through building a sound financial house. She helps families determine if they are properly protected and strive for financial and debt independence. Zenobia is honored to be part of a business that helps families reach their goals and dreams, creating an unbreakable bond that connects clients, representatives, and the company through faith, hope, and enthusiasm.

## Pastor Hakeem J. Webb

Hakeem J. Webb is the founder and senior pastor of Kingdom Business International Ministries (KBIM) in Spring Hill, Tennessee. With more than ten years in ministry, Hakeem is committed to teaching and preaching the gospel of salvation. Hakeem is co-founder and CEO of National Christian Financial Advisors, Inc. (NCFA) with over fifteen years of service and retail and institutional wealth management experience to ministries and families. The principal focus of NCFA is to help the Body of Christ create, preserve, and distribute wealth for its families and heirs by developing and maintaining long-term relationships through excellence, faith, integrity, and exceptional client satisfaction. NCFA provides Bible-based financial consulting services and compliance in the areas of 401(a), 403(b) and 401-K. Hakeem has an M.S. degree in financial services and several leading financial industry designations. He is the author of several books, including *Money, Success and Wealth Seminar System*, which teaches believers how to manage their money from Biblical and practical perspectives.

# Prayers

**My Prayer**

I pray this book will be an added blessing to help you gain knowledge to embrace your singleness and prepare you for that special mate the Lord has in store for you. Below are scriptures that reflect on true love, the type of love you need in your life to be a reflection of Christ, His heart for His children.

[7] *Dear friends, let us love one another, because love comes from God. Everyone who loves has been born again because of what God has done. That person knows God.* [8] *Anyone who does not love does not know God, because God is love.* [9] *How did God show His love for us? He sent his one and only Son into the world. He sent him so we could receive life through him.* [10] *What is love? It is not that we loved God. It is that He loved us and sent His Son to give his life to pay for our sins.* [11] *Dear friends, since God loved us that much, we should also love one another.* [12] *No one has ever seen God. But if we love one another, God lives in us. His love is made complete in us. (1 John 4: 7-12)*

*Prayer by Prophetess Pamela Whatley of GLU Ministries, Birmingham, Alabama*

Dear Lord,

We pray that the words in this anointed book will be a blessing to all readers. My prayer is that your wisdom, knowledge, and understanding transform deep into the hearts that need and accept this project. Let each word purify and shed light through your anointed power. Holy Spirit, each time this book is read, we speak that lives will be changed and transformed. The faith that is being released is not behind us, but it is For Now, Right Now, Healing, Right Now Deliverance, and Right Now Forgiveness. Right Now is the time. To let go of the past, you will move forward and become whole again. Again I say, "Wait on the Lord in Jesus name." Amen

## Husband and Wife Prayers

### By Deacon Anthony and Sister Denise Reed

### A Prayer for Marriage

We pray, LORD, that you will enable us to honor You by submitting to one another. *May You, who give patience, faithfulness and encouragement, help us to live in complete harmony with each other; each with the attitude of Christ toward one another (Romans. 15:5). As a result, may we live happily in Your love through all the days of our life (Ecclesiastes.9:9).*

*LORD, we will not get weary in prayer but keep praying and watching for Your answers (Colossians.4:2). We shall keep on rejoicing in You, for we know that as we love You and pray for one another, that the Holy Spirit will help us; for everything works to the good of those that love the LORD (Romans. 8:28).*

*Glory be unto You, God, who by Your mighty power at work in this our marriage is able to do far more than we could ask or even dream of beyond our highest prayers, desires, hopes or thoughts. Glory to You through endless ages (Ephesians. 3:20-21). Amen.*

### A Prayer for My Husband or Wife

#### The Mind

*LORD, I pray that my spouse will have the rich experience of knowing Christ with certainty and clear understanding. Your plan for him/her is Christ Himself, and in Him are contained all the treasures of wisdom and knowledge (Colossians. 2:2-3). May he/she not be carnally minded, which is death, but spiritually minded, which is life and peace (Romans. 8:6). Bring into captivity his/her every thought to the obedience of Christ (II Corinthians. 10:5).*

*LORD, I pray that you fill his/her thoughts with heaven so that he/she does not spend time worrying about earthly things (Colossians. 3:2). Fix his/her thoughts on what is true and good and right. May he/she think about things that are pure and lovely and dwell on the good things in others; rejoicing in every good thing you have done (Philippians.4:8). I pray that he/she will not be conformed to the things of this world, but that he/she will be transformed by the renewing of his/her mind; so that he/she may know what is the good, acceptable and perfect will of the LORD (Romans . 12:2).*

### The Eyes

*LORD, I pray that You open his/her eyes that he/she may truly see from your perspective (II Kings. 6:17). FATHER, keep his/her eyes alert for spiritual danger, stand true to You, be Your man/woman and be strong (1 Corinthians. 16:13-14). Help him/her to watch out for the snares of Satan, our great enemy (1 Peter. 5:8).*

### The Ears

*FATHER, Your word says that faith comes by hearing and hearing by Your word (Romans. 10:17). I pray that my husband/wife will hear Your words with his/her heart. Speak again and again Father, open his/her ears and grant wisdom, causing a knowing of Your mind. I pray that he/she will listen and not resist or turn away from You (Isaiah. 50:5).*

### The Mouth

Lord, You gave us two ears and one mouth; therefore it was meant for us to listen twice as much as we speak, so that when our mouths are open our words carry wisdom *(Proverbs. 15:2 & 18:15)*. Grant to *him/her* boldness in testimony *(Acts 4:29, Ephesians. 6:19)*. Let *his/her* conversation be gracious and wise, for then *he/she* will have the right answers for everyone *(Colossians. 3:17 & 4:3-6)*. Father, help *him/her* not to complain or argue *(Philippians. 2:14)*. *Lord, I pray that we talk to each other much about You; quoting psalms and hymns and singing sacred songs, making music in our hearts to exhalt You (Ephesians. 5:19-21). Let the words of our mouths and the meditation of our hearts be acceptable unto You, O LORD (Psalm. 19:14).*

### The Heart

*Lord, I pray that You enable my spouse to obey Your command which is to love the LORD, our GOD, with all of our heart and with all of our soul and with all of his/her might (Deuteronomy. 6:5 & Matt. 22:37-40). Let his/her heart be filled with You alone to make (him/her) pure and true (James. 4:8). Create in (him/her) a clean heart, O God, filled with clean thoughts and right desires (Psalm. 51:10). A new heart will You give him/her and a new spirit; whereby You will take away the stony heart and in return give a heart of flesh and You shall pour out Your spirit that he/she may walk in Your statutes is Your promise, Father (Ezekiel. 36:26-27).*

*Cause him/her to trust in You, Lord, with all of his/her heart and lean not unto his/her own understanding (Proverbs. 3:5). May we worship You and serve You with a clean heart and a willing mind, for You see our hearts and know our every thought (I Chronicles. 28:9).*

*Finally, Lord, I pray that You will let Your peace rule in our hearts (Colossians. 3:15). I pray that Christ will be more and more at home in his/her heart as he/she trusts You more and more.*

*Glory be unto You, God, who by Your mighty power at work in this our marriage are able to do far more than we could ask or even dream of beyond our highest prayers, desires, hopes, or thoughts. Glory to You through endless ages (Ephesians. 3:20-21). Amen.*

# 1

# *Embracing Your Singleness*

It may be difficult for someone to grasp that he or she is single. Two reasons are fear of being alone and the need to be in a relationship for the sense of validation from his or her partner. These are the wrong reasons to enter into any relationship.

Ask yourself these questions: Why is it so hard for me to embrace being single? Don't I want to wait for God's best selection for my life?

If you answered yes to the last question, it's time to embrace *you* and to realize that being single has been the best time in your life, because you have now submitted to God's plan instead of your own.

*I truly have been blessed. The Lord has dealt with me as an individual on how to become a better woman, mother, daughter, and friend, and to prepare me one day again to be a wife. He continues to bring forth things about me; each day the process becomes easier. I receive wholeness in my life from my Father. I embrace the time even more to pray, fast, and get into His presence. And now, being able to go before Him without spot or blemish, I learned my self-worth and value as His daughter to honor Him and my temple.*

So today, my fellow brother or sister, embrace being single so He can prepare you to be a better woman or man of God.

Below are testimonies, prayers, and affirmations to assist you each day during your singleness until you are joined together with your spouse chosen by God.

*Testimony-Mimi in Waterbury, Connecticut*

I am known as MiMi. I am 53 years old and have been divorced for 28 years. I would like to say that I have been celibate all those years, but I can't. I can say that I have been celibate for the past 14 years. I was not always the Woman of God I am today; if I can do it, you can too. Not on your own but with God's help every step of the way. Therefore, I did not have to think I had the "goods" – I *had* the "goods." This did not pump up my head, but I had to take a long look at things. I was in an adulterous relationship and knew I had to get out. I remembered the old adage, "Why buy the cow when you can get the milk for free?" Since the man I was involved with did not want to "buy the cow," I had to say goodbye.

I knew I was saved, yet my flesh still called yearned for what it always had on those Friday nights. I wanted to live a life that was pleasing to God. I could not cheat on Him any longer.

I took a crash course at Oral Roberts University during a pilgrimage to Tulsa, Oklahoma, for a conference, titled "Purity with a Purpose – Experiencing Secondary Virginity." It changed my life. The class inspired me to read as many chapters of the Bible regarding fornication, adultery, abstinence, and purity so that I could be delivered. I did this daily until I totally surrendered to God.

**How do I do this abstaining thing?**

- Pray to God asking Him to take away the desire for sex and love-making until the appointed time, meaning marriage.
- Make a vow to God that you will not entertain your flesh.
- Keep your vow (but know if you fall, You will repent and get up and keep going forward).
- Be comfortable with who you are and whose you are in Christ Jesus.
- Know that every man you meet is not for you and does not always want you in any way other than a friend.
- Do not allow yourself to be caught in compromising positions.
- Monitor your eye gate: Be careful what you view on TV or videos. Often just a glimpse can make Your body go into orbit.
- Monitor your ear gate: Often music can and will cause you to "remember the time…"
- Monitor conversations with males who are just friends that I call the "row- boat factor." This is when you talk about anything and

everything under the sun. When you realize that you have rowed out too far, pick up those oars and row back to shore (change the subject).

- Ask God for a mate.
- When you do meet the man God has sent into your life, listen to what he is saying. Often, as women, we move too fast. He may have high standards, and you bedding him down could make him flee. Some men as well are saving themselves for marriage.
- When you meet that man of God, pray and be thankful for the gift and *only* worship the Giver.

As SINGLES, we should embrace this season. Why? We have such an advantage over married couples. At any moment of the day or night, God can call upon us to pray in our prayer language, sing, worship, or write. We can do this without interrupting anyone. We can volunteer our time and not be asked, "Honey, what time will you be coming home?" I am speaking to those with no children or grown children.

If you are raising small children, things will be different. Raising small children is your ministry. Therefore, know your limit. You want to pray, sing, worship, or write when God nudges you. It will be rewarding. Each morning at 5:00, I am up praying, reading the Bible and taking Holy Communion with Him. I anticipate the time God will nudge me. Doing so has allowed me to be minister to God's women, whether it is at a Women's Conference in Southbury, Connecticut, at 7:00 P.M. or on the warm sands on the beach of Maui, Hawaii, at 7:00 A.M.

Through all of this, I have become extremely confident in *who* I am and *whose* I am in Christ Jesus. I have, therefore, embraced this season of singleness because I believe God has someone for me, and because God has been so good to me. I actually want for nothing. I want to continue to please Him in all that I do. My time is given to ministering to women who are battered, homeless, incarcerated, or transitioning from the prison system back into society. I also prepare messages for a conference call ministry to Ghana Africa, Nigeria, London, Jamaica, and the United States, as well as some first ladies, pastors, and bishops.

This walk with Jesus is the best thing that has ever happened to me. I pray that you are encouraged to let go and let God have His way in your life of singleness. By loving Him, you can begin to love yourself. Then you can love others and ultimately the mate that God has prepared for you. We have had it backwards for so long.

### Testimony-TR in Birmingham, Alabama

My dear people of God, so many times we go through this life thinking, "I need to be married to be or feel complete." One whole man plus one whole woman equals one unity in God's eyes. On my 40th birthday, I had a rude awakening. After my party, I went to my hotel room alone, by my choice. I could have invited some guy to go with me, but the truth is, that's just a booty call. At first it seemed strange, but it allowed me to be free of the feeling that I needed someone else to make me whole. It was lonesome, but I made it through the night. These are the things that will make you stronger than you can imagine. It was years before I realized that I can live a pure, sex-free life and still be joyful. (I ate a lot of chocolate the first year.) God's blessings are sure. Wait on the Lord; he has the best in store for you. Yes, you can make it. Yes, you can in Christ!

### Prayer for Single Man or Woman

Dear Heavenly Father, thank you that the source of my being is from You. *(Romans 9:16)* As I walk into this day and accept being single, please keep my mind and thoughts pure at all times. *(Hebrews 9:14, 10:22, 2 Corinthians 10:5, Ephesians 6:12)* Lord, I know I am not perfect, but I am striving for perfection daily. Lord, please give me a heart of humbleness and a willingness to accept things that are true and that may be my own flaws or bad habits so I may work on changing for the better. *(1 Peter 5:6-8)* Lord, I don't want to fall into a prideful way of thinking and miss out on the blessings that You have in store for me because I failed to change and listen to direction from You. *(James 4:6)* Help me accept being single and whole and to understand that you are working on me. I refrain from thinking that I need someone in my life to fulfill a void or loneliness.

Lord, I find it hard at times to accept being single, but this is the time for me to shine, so please teach me to wait on You and the destiny that You have planned for my life concerning the spouse You have chosen just for me. During my time of being single, teach me to be patient and not to make false moves by being in a relationship before the time You have spoken. *(Isaiah 25:1, Galatians 6:9, Matthew 7:24)*

I am being critiqued by you to become the best wife or husband I can be. I am married to You during this time so when I'm presented to my spouse, the values of a wife or husband will be instilled in me, and in Your perfect timing I will be joined together with the spouse You have ordained for my life. Strengthen me, oh, Father, in the areas of my life that I have admitted weakness.

Satan, you are now placed on notice because I openly admit to the Lord my struggles, and He will grant me my strength. *(Matthew 24:12-13, Psalm 28:7)*

Father, as I learn to live a life of wholeness, I vow not to commit the sin of fornication or adultery. This is not Your will, and I only want to do what is pleasing in Your sight. Teach me to become that woman of virtue or Man of Valor. Help me stand strong and bold in You, so my values of life will only be from the book of life, the Bible. *(1 Thessalonians 4:3-8, Leviticus 11:44-45, 1 John 3: 2-3, 1 Corinthians 6:18-20, Proverbs 6:32)*

Lord, my being and purpose are to be a servant and the best daughter or son that you have molded me to become. Lord, I walk this life with You without a spot or blemish, so whatever I ask in Your name it shall be granted because of my faith and obedience in You. *(Genesis 17:1)*

As I speak this prayer, Lord, release Your glory in my life. Father, you receive all the praise, the glory, and the honor. *(Psalm 8:1)*

In the Name of Jesus Christ of Nazareth, Amen.

## *Affirmations for Purity*

Scripture references: *(Psalm 16:18, Numbers 30 3-8, Hebrews 13:4)*

**I vow** I am a virtuous woman.

**I vow** I am a man of valor.

**I vow** I am a woman of integrity.

**I vow** I am a man of wisdom and knowledge.

**I vow** my temple is holy for the Lord.

**I vow** that before I enter into a relationship I have received clearance and direction from my Father in Heaven.

**I vow** I am worth the wait.

**I vow** to remain a virgin or abstain from premarital sex until I am joined together with my God-given spouse.

**I vow** to reject any sexual advances or entertain any conversation about sex with anyone other than my God-given spouse.

**I vow** that I am empowered with knowledge about the sin of fornication and how it displeases the Lord.

**I vow** that I am kingdom child who has Godly principals instilled in my life.

# 2

# I Really Want To Be Married

*Proverbs 18:22 He who finds a wife finds a good thing and obtains favor from the Lord. When a man finds a wife, he finds a good thing.*

Ladies, before he found you, you were already a good thing in the sight of our Father. This scripture is powerful because it shows you how the Lord honors union between a man and a woman. The man obtains favor from the Lord. He found you, and the Lord grants him favor.

As women, we often dream about our wedding day. This vision starts as little girls when we are playing house with our dolls, imagining we are Cinderella and Prince Charming sweeps us off our feet. Sometimes while watching movies or sitcoms showing positive images of wonderful marriages, you may think, "I really want to be married and I desire this type of marriage."

You can pray for marriage as healthy and beautiful as Christ intended it to be, but the key is listening to the Lord and hearing who He has chosen for your mate. This decision is not for you to make; seek direction from God. We trust God to make most of our decisions, but when it comes to relationships, we often forget He is there and wonder why we are left broken-hearted and hurt. Why? Because we did not follow His direction. His ways are always pure and perfect.

Before you get married, you need to do self-evaluation. Ask, Am I embracing being single? Do I want to be married because I see that others are? Examine your relationships that have ended. Ask God if this is the season for you to be married. That is the key; once you have received God's answer you will know where you stand. *Your* timeline is not God's timeline. Remember God's alignment and plan.

For example, you receive news from your best friend that she is getting married. You act happy, but inside you feel jealous because you really want to be married. She asks you to assist in planning her big day. The wedding day is finally here. The music is playing. You see your best friend walk down the aisle in her beautiful dress. You want to be happy for her, but you feel disappointed and wonder when it is going to happen for you. (Stop thinking about it and allow the Lord to guide the timing of your Boaz. Remember, He will find you.)

Your thoughts continue. "I'll be a great wife. We will go on vacations and attend functions together." You are having wrong thoughts. You need to be attentive and remember that the reason you are there is to celebrate your friend's day. You need to be happy for her and her husband as they embark on a blessed union together.

As asked before, Am I embracing being single? Do I want to be married because everyone else is? You have to be honest with yourself and God. Marriage is not a union to be entered into lightly. Marriage is a beautiful covenant honored by God. Most people desire true wedded bliss, but in the meantime, embrace being single and submit unto the Lord as your husband.

So when it is your time, everyone will be standing as you walk down the aisle in your beautiful white gown to greet the husband designed especially for you by God.

The following testimony speaks to the importance of waiting for God's plan to receive the gift of a strong marriage.

### Testimony-Ms. G in West Palm Beach, Florida

Every girl dreams about her wedding day and does not realize how much work it takes to have a good marriage. When I was only eighteen years old, I was a college student living in West Palm Beach, Florida. I learned the essence of being established first and then working on family. Moving back to Atlanta, Georgia, this was not a focal point. It was like a culture shock. The trend in West Palm Beach was to get married really young and have children, as while in Atlanta, marriage is not even a thought. I believe the media and Southern tradition have influenced this trend. Now I am twenty-two years old and believe there's more to marriage then sex. My beliefs stem from my parents, who have been happily married for 23 years. Marriage is not as easy as it seems, but my parents are truly in love. My parents taught me that when two people share true love before and during marriage and sex is not the main appeal, making love with your mate after marriage will be more sensual and meaningful.

I would like a relationship with a good foundation, like my parents have. They are best friends who share common interests. My parents always told me that the keys to a successful relationship are communication, patience, being best friends, maturity, and understanding. They said it was important that the man you choose treats his mother and grandmother with respect.

If the man finds you, and he possesses all the qualities you are looking for and respects the women in his life, he is a keeper. Marry for the right reasons, because you love the person and can see yourself with him or her. Physical attraction may fade; friendship and love will not.

# 3

# *Getting To Know Me and You*

## *Selection of a Mate Chosen by God*

To allow Your Father to choose the mate for you, the decision has to be made on a spiritual and intellectual level, not an emotional one, not out of lust or a fear of being alone. *During this time, the Lord is preparing you to guard your heart. The heart is deceitful above all things and beyond cure. (Jeremiah 17:9)*

Your heart can overtake you, causing you not to think rationally and intelligently, so you must leave the selection to the Lord. The Lord wants us to follow the design of being friends first, courting, and then marriage.

Friendship is developed through learning, growing, taking time to listen, being supportive, celebrating your friend's victories, and providing words of encouragement. It is important to share common interests and values, have similar spiritual walks, and eat from the same bread of life. If you are seeking friendship, courtship, and marriage, and if the person is not seeking the same interests as you are, then you know he or she is not the person God has in store for you. If a gentleman or lady states that he or she is not looking for a serious relationship, take his/her words as being open and honest and be respectful of what he/she is expressing. Don't try to persuade him/her; that will be pressuring him/her into a relationship for which he/she is not ready. *He who finds a wife finds a good thing and received favor from the Lord. The word of God didn't say she who finds, it's clear in all translations of the bible he that finds. (Proverbs 18:22)*

In the beginning, God created Adam and took the rib of Adam to provide him a helpmate; woman (Eve) was formed. You are Eve to your Adam, and he will recognize you. Ladies, allow a man to be the man. Allow him to take the lead in the relationship, because ultimately he is the head of the household. A man of valor will be directed by God concerning destiny and purpose. If he struggles, he is confused and not certain of his mission. He has not sought after the plan God has designed for his life.

Finally, pray about him having a healthy love and acceptance for himself, meaning he has taken time to heal from past relationships and made peace with God and himself. His walk with God is crucial, meaning he is appreciative in all areas of his life and he admires the beauty of God's creations, such as trees, flowers, birds, and especially *you*. Unhealthy life cycles that can affect men are drama, problem making commitments, frequent mood swings, not taking ownership of problems, blaming others, and not keeping promises. Ask, is he a man of integrity? Ask God to help you recognize the unhealthy cycles he may be struggling with and if he has accepted deliverance. Do not hastily decide based upon what looks wonderful. Many men are hurting and have not allowed the Lord to make them whole, to heal the wounds of broken relationships.

## Get to Know Each Other

Before the minister pronounces you husband and wife, know *you*. Women often picture the type of husband they want: tall, handsome, smart, great career, family-oriented, etc. Pray to the Lord; He knows who will be best for you.

When you wait on the Lord for your mate, Satan assigns agents to stop what God has in place. *No weapon formed against Me shall prosper, and every tongue which rises against Me in judgment you shall condemn. (Isaiah 54:17)*

Ask the Lord for discernment to uncover those agents so you won't waste your time. The Lord will give you details concerning your mate. The Lord will summon your heart and tell you when it's time for you to date and how long you should remain single. While you are waiting, He will help you get ready for your mate spiritually, mentally, and emotionally, and enrich your spirit, mind, and body.

*Again I say to you, if two of you agree on earth about anything they ask, it will be done for them by My Father in heaven. For where two or three are gathered in My name, there am I among them. (Matthew 18: 19-20) Do two walk together unless they have agreed to do so. (Amos 3:3)* Those two powerful scriptures will bless your friendship, courtship, and marriage to walk together in unity.

When you begin dating, allow God to provide you with the questions that you want to ask regarding your relationship.

Strive to have the same expectations and goals for the future, but know that the common denominator is the Lord. You and your mate should share the same feelings and beliefs about your relationship. *The word of God speaks about being unequally yoked. Do not be unequally yoked together with unbelievers. For what fellowship has righteousness with the lawless? And what communion has light with darkness? (2 Corinthians 6:14)*

Consider if you are complementing one another regarding your talents and gifts, and if you are blessing others with your fellowship together. Also consider these questions to see if you are equally yoked: How strong is your relationship with the Lord? Do you put the Lord on the back burner during the week, and then pick Him back up on Sunday?

Ladies, make sure your ear gates are open to listen because the answers to your questions will be presented to you if you pay attention. Men love when a woman is attentive to them in conversation and allow them to speak. Pray that he will be open and honest with you, but keep in mind that no one is perfect. Do not complain, nag, or be negative. Do not bring up past relationships. If you do, a man may flee. If you fall short in any of these areas, ask the Lord to bring forth your deliverance. Remember, God is molding us daily into His image for His Glory.

We often have high expectations, but fail to ask the Father what his expectations are or if this is the person He has chosen for us. When we do this, we suffer great disappointment and brokenness because we chose this person for ourselves instead of waiting for the Lord to reveal His choice.

Ladies, trust in the Lord in all areas of your life, especially regarding your mate. He is not a failing God. His ways are good and excellent every time. That is something to celebrate. The key to getting to know one another is to develop boundaries in your relationship.

Getting to know one another is fun; you are uncovering mysteries about the other person. As you begin dating, you are learning more about that person. That learning continues even after years of marriage.

## Stories

### Toni

It is amazing when the Lord gives you a peace and joy in your spirit.

Toni was in a broken state of mind. She had just separated from her husband after committing adultery.

Toni's father was never part of her life. He had another family. Her mom was a single parent, and other family members had helped raise her. Toni never lacked for anything. She always had material things, but the one thing she missed was a father's love. At the age of sixteen, Toni began dating drug dealers who could provide for her.

Her mother worked and her family never had time for her. Toni wanted to be in the house of the Lord at an early age. She knew the Lord, but never fully accepted him until later in life. No one ever explained to her that she should wait until she was married to have sex, to share this special gift with her husband. Brokenness started early in her life. She had one relationship after another without taking the time to heal.

At the age of eighteen, she got pregnant. Her family was very disappointed; they had big plans for her. Toni tried to build a relationship with her child's father, Jackson, but he didn't want anything to do with her and the baby. Toni struggled with raising the baby, working and finishing college. She soon began another relationship and moved in with her new boyfriend. She believed she was on the right track, but her values were wrong. She forgot about her responsibilities.

Realizing the relationship was ending, she began a new relationship with a married man and got pregnant again. Steven asked Toni to get an abortion. She thought about it, but decided to keep the baby. Neither child's father was a part of their lives.

Toni finished her degree and received a great job. She thought she had her priorities in order, but unhealthy relationships were her weakness. She never took time to evaluate why she ended up in broken relationships.

Toni did not foresee the problems ahead. She never took the time to get to know herself. She continued to waste her time on relationships that went nowhere, never healing from the mental and emotional stress of her relationships.

Toni realized that she needed to be closer to the Lord. She went back to church and was on the right path. She stopped dating for nearly eight months to take time to heal. When she thought she was ready to start dating again, she met Shawn. Toni felt he was a perfect match because he attended church regularly. After a few months they were married, but Toni had not seen that Shawn was an abuser. She was terrified that he would abuse her, and he did. She later found out he had been arrested for domestic violence on several occasions.

Toni repeated a cycle of not getting to know herself or her mate. She jumped in too quickly to satisfy a need to be married before first healing from her previous relationship. Toni was in a denial state of mind, not willing to accept anyone's help. Toni wanted someone to love her the way Christ loves her.

Toni divorced Shawn and is doing well, taking time to enjoy the Lord. She realized the importance of examining herself in order to receive what

God has planned for her. Toni is waiting on the Lord to send the mate that He designed especially for her.

<u>April</u>

April was well known in school and had the nice-looking boyfriends, but could not stay in a relationship longer than six months. She never took the time to examine why she couldn't maintain a meaningful relationship.

April's problem may have stemmed from the void she felt and the fact that she was operating in a lust spirit. Her situation is called lust verses love.

April was giving her virtue to men who didn't respect her, and she was not able to tell if a real man approached her because of the spirit in which she was operating. April's dad often traveled and her Mom worked. When her dad would come home, he would lock himself in a room and not to come out for hours. Once in the middle of the night, the door of that room was open and April saw her dad watching x-rated movies. She was so disappointed in her father.

One day, she came home and found her dad having sex with another woman. She ran out of the house in tears. She couldn't talk about the incident for years.

Years later, April married. For seven years she had a great marriage until she found her husband watching pornography, speaking with women on the chat line, and sending pornographic photos. She said she knew he had this problem before they were married, that they would often watch pornography together. She had invited this spirit into her marriage and God was not pleased with this behavior. April and her husband had invited Satan. Her husband began to have affairs, and April did not understand why. April agreed to seek God and counseling and asked how she could be saved, delivered, and set free. She and her husband are now serving God with fullness and loving hearts. Their marriage is even stronger than before they invited the Lord in. They overcame the obstacles together, and now they are counseling other couples facing trouble in their marriage.

Many people are broken or lost and don't know where to turn. Seek someone who will accept you for who you are and not try to change you, someone who uplifts and encourages you and shares a common love, which is Jesus Christ.

We are all works in progress. If someone asks you to have a fling, know that this is not what God intended for you. Wait to have excitement with your spouse; you will be blessed by God.

Women were made to be helpmates for their husbands. Women are nurturers and bearers of life. The Lord has poured grace, beauty, and wisdom into all his daughters, who are pleasing to the Lord and to their husbands-to-be.

Ladies, every man you come in contact with does not want to marry you. Allow God to show you who that special person will be. *He that foundeth a wife, that means not you to find him, please let's stay in order. (Proverbs 18:22)* Wait on the Lord; He knows what is best for you. If you are seeking to be married, establish your relationship with God first. He is your husband while you are single, so do not lose sight of God.

## *Key points in this chapter:*

- Get to know God and ask Him to evaluate you.
- If you are seeking a marriage or relationship, pray, asking if you are ready.
- Get to know if the person you are in a relationship with is for you.
- If you seek to be married, speak with a Christian relationship counselor to address situations that you may be unaware of.
- Always pray for one another and give respect, support, and encouragement.
- Be best friends with your mate.

## *Testimony- I-Charity in Atlanta, Georgia*

My mother raised me in the church, but the church wasn't in me. At the age of 17, I accepted Jesus as my Lord and Savior. Shortly after that, I married my husband after one year of dating. I knew nothing about marriage, but I knew I didn't want to live in sin. My husband and I decided to get saved. As the Bible says, *"Be ye not unequally yoked together with unbelievers: for what fellowship hath righteousness with unrighteousness? And what communion hath like with darkness?" (2 Corinthians 6:14.)* For us to be as one, we would have to be equally yoked. I moved out of my mother's house and moved in with my husband's family, not knowing he had been brought up in a Christian home. As I got to know my mother-in-law, many things were revealed to me about my husband that I had been unaware of.

Two years later, I got pregnant with a baby girl and had a miscarriage. From that point on, my husband began abusing me mentally, physically, and emotionally. I didn't understand what I had done to deserve it. I had done everything I knew I was supposed to do as a wife. I often prayed, but things got worse. It became too much to handle and I began to go stray from the Lord's will and allow the enemy to take control. I decided to leave my husband.

I turned to alcohol and drugs to ease the pain. My spirit had died. I committed adultery and was pregnant again. Three months after delivering my baby boy, he died. The drugs were devouring me.

After two years of separation, I divorced my husband. I went through trials and tribulations, but through it all, He kept me and gave me another chance. I am born again believer and now I'm set free. I am greater, better, and wiser. For those who desire to be married......"*Trust in the Lord with all thine heart; and lean not unto thine own understanding.*" *(Proverbs 3:5).*

## Testimony-True Foundation in Charleston, South Carolina

Marriage is a sacred union between a man and woman that is honored by the Lord. A marriage should honor God first and friendship second. A husband and wife should share everything. They should celebrate, compliment, encourage, and love each other. Never go to bed angry; talk about your situation calmly.

I married someone I thought was my true love. But as time went by, he presented his true person to me. He was self-absorbed, which hurt our marriage. This is a pride issue, and God is against this spirit. It hurt that he was not who he presented himself to be (false image).

You can tell how a man will treat you by the way he treats the other women in his family. I ignored every sign given to me because I was praying that my husband would change. Then came the battle of verbal abuse and mistrust.

I took a stand for the Lord. Today my husband and I are separated because the foundation of our marriage was built on a lie. I thank God that He saved me from an unstable marriage. I have not looked back. I look forward to doing God's will and asking for my true Boaz.

## Testimony-Still Learning in Atlanta, Georgia

Being divorced has taught me that, no matter what, you have to seek God's face in every situation. You have to learn not only to talk to your spouse, but to be in constant communication with your Heavenly Father. Going to friends and relatives is not the best choice. Fasting and staying in constant prayer affords the opportunity to hear God clearly. Strive each day to be a true reflection of Christ, loving unconditionally even when it hurts.

## A Forgiving Heart in Atlanta, Georgia

Over twenty years ago, I met my husband. I thought I had hit the jackpot! God was smiling on me. My handsome, intelligent husband was a crack addict and I, being a naive young woman, had no idea of the drama that was going to unfold. He did not pay the bills or take care of us. He pawned our only car and stole and sold items in our house. He took our children with him to buy drugs.

The last straw was taking my wedding ring off my finger, against my will, to pawn it for $75.00. I finally gave up after three years. For fifteen years, we didn't see or hear from him. I knew he went to jail numerous times.

My heart was broken. I immersed myself in the Word of God, and prayed more. Slowly I forgave, just as God forgives us. I had to forgive him in order to move on. Many nights I cried myself to sleep. Twenty years later, my oldest son saw him in a store and he didn't even recognize his own son. We all reconnected and decided to give it another shot: After all, we loved each other way back then, and he had been clean for several years and had a good job. We got back together and got reacquainted. It was exciting to be a family again. The boys enjoyed having their father around again, and I enjoyed having my husband again loving, affectionate, supportive, and kind. We are no longer together, but I learned from this experience to have a forgiving heart.

# 4

# I Will Wait On My "Godly" Spouse

## By Lady M and Yolanda Marshall

When a woman is approached by a married man, how should she handle the situation? Ask yourself: Are you a woman of integrity or of foolishness? If a man approaches you and tells you he is married but having problems and planning to divorce his wife, tell him you will keep him lifted in your prayers.

The Lord is against the adulterous spirit. A woman of integrity knows her boundaries; she will not enter into a relationship with a married man. She fears God and knows the word. She is aware of the consequences of being in that type of relationship. She values herself, the wife, and the family that this would hurt.

A foolish woman doesn't care who it hurts. This woman is competing against the wife and trying to destroy the covenant of marriage.

It is not God's plan for you to have a relationship with a married man. Many people are trapped in a situation like this because the other person lied about his or her marital status.

Pray before entering into any relationship and wait for the Lord to give you the answer. There are reasons the Lord does not give you an answer right away. He is about to show you something.

It is important for those who are praying and fasting to wait for the Lord to bless them with the spouse that He has for them. The Word of God says, *Rest in the Lord, and wait patiently for him. (Psalm 37:7).* God hears your prayers; continue to delight yourself in the Lord. Your desire for a spouse will soon manifest. You are in the "best season" of your life. Declare and know the man or woman is coming.

## God Will Send My Husband to Me

My pastor always said, "Single ladies, make yourselves available and continue to serve God faithfully. The man of God will find you. When you as a single woman allow God to prepare you for marriage, trust that He will let His chosen man find you.

When you let God send Him to you, you will no longer need to entertain negative thoughts. Often we miss our blessing because of our fear of being hurt. Some women think that men are "all the same." This can also hinder her from receiving the right man. If you have these feelings, ask God to help you so you will not take them into your marriage.

Continue to serve God when your husband arrives. Don't forget the One who sent him to you. Always stay focused on what God has called you to do.

## God Will Bless Me to Find My Wife

There is a song that says, "God favored me." Men, it is an awesome experience to have favor with God. It is truly a blessing to find that beautiful, intelligent, God-fearing, virtuous woman. Only God can prepare woman for you. It was all in God's perfect plan to create a virtuous woman to walk by your side.

While you search for your wife, continue to seek God's face. When God blesses you to find her, do not be concerned about what your friends say. Your only concern should be for the rib (woman) with which God has blessed you for the purpose of ministry.

Your wife needs to know that she has a husband who is "committed and submitted" to God—one who not only goes to church, but has the love of God in his heart. Once you find that wife, and she sees your love for God, she can trust your unconditional love for her. *Husbands love your wives, even as Christ also loved the church, and gave himself for it. (Ephesians 5:25)*

Single men, it is your responsibility to respect and love your mate/wife. Observe how you treat women now. When a man does not respect women, he can miss his blessing (potential wife).

## *Why Did That Married Woman Approach Me?*

Many single men are approached by carnal-minded married women with ungodly motives. Some of them may reveal that they are married; some may not.

A married woman who seeks anyone but her husband is not virtuous. She may be neglected at home and feel she would gain what she needs by having a man on the side. This is the enemy's trick.

Single men, ask yourselves the following questions: Is this married woman worth damaging my relationship with God? Should I compromise my godly standards for this woman? How would I feel if I were this woman's husband and learned she was seeking someone else? Could I trust her if she left her husband for me? What would Jesus do?

If you know that a woman who approaches you is married, it is your responsibility to go in a different direction. When you fear the Lord, you can easily turn away. Don't be moved by what you see. Pray, walk in integrity, and use the wisdom of God.

# 5

# *Words of Wisdom*

This section is about your feelings of self-worth as a woman of virtue, dealing with the issues of hurt in a relationship, determining if a man has a fear of commitment, and recognizing if a relationship is built on lust or love. It will help you to fulfill God's promises regarding marriage.

## *My Pearl*

A woman's pearl is God's gift to women that makes them different from men. Women are nurturers and bearers of love and life. The Lord made every woman special and unique, so she must be careful when giving her pearl. Every man is not deserving. Do not compromise your faith and destabilize your walk if he is leading you into sexual sin, causing distraction from your commitment to God. Your relationship with the Father is of value and love, so do not offend God. A man of valor will recognize you as a pearl of great value and be willing to do whatever he must to win you. God honors being a virgin; He will reward your commitment to keeping this vow for your chosen husband. You will walk with the Lord and He will direct you to the right pathway. Keep your pearl sacred and secure until your honeymoon night and you will understand His purpose and experience the beauty of unveiling your pearl to your husband.

## *Testimony-My Self-Worth in New York, New York*

As a young lady, I had a desire to be married, but I took wrong turns in my life, causing me to become hurtful and broken. Not having a clue that I was involved in the wrong relationships, I gave my virtue to someone not worthy of it. I realized that this was becoming a cycle; I was getting into relationships without consulting the Lord. I thought I knew it all, but I was acting foolishly. So the cycle continued relationship after relationship, with different men but the same qualities. I didn't realize that something was going on inside that I needed to pay attention to.

I knew the heavenly Father, but my relationship with the Lord was not as strong because of my disobedience. As I attended church more, I was often surrounded by women who were virgins, abstaining until the Lord sent forth a husband. I was being taught to save myself for my husband. As my relationship with the Lord developed, things started to change around me. I put away childish things and became what He summoned me to be, a virtuous woman. I now know the importance of saving myself until I am married. The Lord healed me and instructed me not to go into a relationship with hurt, anger, or bitterness until he releases me to do so. Now I understand why I was surrounded by women who were obedient and pure. He has the ultimate plan for my life with the mate He designed especially for me. The Lord imparted knowledge to me, first on being a virtuous woman ready to receive what He has designed for me. The Lord showed me that marriage takes work by two imperfect people coming together to share, unite, honor, be joyous, compromise, and have a relationship with the Lord.

## Hurt Versus Hurt

A hurt person attracts others who are hurting. Ask yourself these questions: How do I know that I am hurting? What type of relationship is considered hurting? How can I keep from being in a hurtful relationship?

Always evaluate yourself to recognize any bitterness, pain, hatred, or resentment that you could be harboring against someone in your past. It's not good to hold on to any of these things. If someone has done something wrong to you, forgive them and release it to the Lord to carry the burden for you. This hurt can grow if it is not addressed at the time of the incident. If you are hurting from an incident that happened in your childhood, it is never too late to address the individual who caused your hurt. Pray to the Lord and ask Him to take the hurt away and give you a heart of forgiveness so peace can enter your life.

I harbored hurt toward my father for over 30 years for not being a part of my life. The Lord asked me if I was willing to let this go. I said yes, and within a year, the Lord allowed me to meet my biological grandfather, who I became close to. I pray my testimony has ministered to your heart to forgive and let God.

How do you know you are in a hurting relationship? One of you is physically or emotionally abusive and you lack respect for one another. You haven't taken time to heal from the past relationship that hurt you. These types of relationships are emotionally draining. It is important after a break up to take time to heal and find yourself so that no hidden hurts come out in your relationship.

How can you keep yourself from being in a hurting relationship? Ask what type of relationship you are seeking. You have the will to leave an unhealthy relationship. If the relationship is hurting in the beginning and you get married, it will become a hurting marriage. Both mates must seek the Lord in His fullness, to be released from any hurt that each have inflicted on the other. Ask the Lord for deliverance. *"Cast your cares on the Lord and he will sustain you." (1 Peter 5:7)*

## The Serial Engager

Ladies, beware of the Serial Engager, the man struggling with the fear of commitment. These men have had a series of engagements. They love the idea of planning a wedding, but when it is time for the big day, they become afraid. Ladies, do you want the disappointment of being left at the altar because he could not go through with the marriage vows? *Lord your God has set the land before you; go up and possess it, as the Lord God of your fathers has spoken to you; do not fear or be discouraged. (Deuteronomy 1:21)*

Fear is not of God. We are not to walk in it, and we are believers that what God has set before you is awesome in His sight. If you are considering someone to be your life-long partner, it is a good idea to seek Christian relationship counseling.

Most men are afraid of commitment. If a man has a genuine love for the Lord, he will treat his mate in a way that is pleasing to the Lord. If the head does not follow instructions from the Lord, he will cause the household to be out of order.

If you are dealing with a fear of commitment, ask the Father for deliverance. The ultimate test is moving fear to faith. Your Faith has designed a plan for you. Receive it and enjoy it!

## Lust Versus Love

**By Former First Lady**

*⁶ When the woman saw that the fruit of the tree was good for food and pleasing to the eye, and also desirable for gaining wisdom, she took some and ate it. She also gave some to her husband, who was with her, and he ate it. (Genesis 3:6)*

Lust is like eating a candy bar when you are a diabetic. The end result is illness and/or death. We know that Satan's job is to kill, steal, and destroy. We know how crafty he is, but his tricks are as old as time. Our natural senses are gifts from God. Our desires and needs were given to us so we would rely upon God and heighten our relationships with each other. If allowed, the evil one takes these desires and needs and misrepresents or twists them into things that are harmful and ungodly. Once these lusts are identified, we should do with them as the Lord instructed Jeremiah to do with the linen sash.

*Thus the LORD said to me: "Go and get yourself a linen sash, and put it around your waist, but do not put it in water." [2] So I got a sash according to the word of the LORD, and put it around my waist.[3] And the word of the LORD came to me the second time, saying, [4] "Take the sash that you acquired, which is around your waist, and arise, go to the Euphrates, and hide it there in a hole in the rock." [5] So I went and hid it by the Euphrates, as the LORD commanded me. [6] Now it came to pass after many days that the LORD said to me, "Arise, go to the Euphrates, and take from there the sash which I commanded you to hide there." [7] Then I went to the Euphrates and dug, and I took the sash from the place where I had hidden it; and there was the sash, ruined. It was profitable for nothing. [8] Then the word of the LORD came to me, saying, [9] "Thus says the LORD: 'In this manner I will ruin the pride of Judah and the great pride of Jerusalem. [10] This evil people, who refuse to hear My words, who follow the dictates of their hearts, and walk after other gods to serve them and worship them, shall be just like this sash which is profitable for nothing."(Jeremiah 13:1-10)*

No one is exempt from the evil one's attempts. This includes every member of every committee, guild, and board in the church. No matter how holy, sanctified, justified, or righteous one believes himself to be, if a door is opened for the evil one to enter, he surely will.

Conversely, unconditional love is the act of giving to and receiving from others the God-given affection, regardless of predisposed attitudes, tendencies, thought processes, and actions. If we strive to be like Jesus, it is imperative that we learn to operate through unconditional love. Godly love is the practice of willfully separating a person and an issue. It is seeing him as Christ sees him and conducting yourself accordingly. We are to pray unceasingly for deliverance, understanding, truth, revelation, honesty, and patience. It takes practice. Seek the will of our Father rather than fulfill the lust of the flesh. When you understand the will of the Father by reading and studying His word, and follow obediently, your discernment will heighten to a level where you can see, hear, and smell the tricks of the enemy before he sets them into motion. Once your discernment is heightened, you will be driven by the Holy Ghost to pray for your spouse and your relationship with God. Do not be fooled by the "goods-looks," smells, tastes good, as was Eve, who shared with Adam. Be virtuous. In a marriage, the main partner must be God. If you must satisfy a lust, let it be a God-given desire to please our Father.

I realized that lust had been at the core of my relationship with my mate from the beginning of our marriage. Lust was painful and tricked us both. I chose not to bow to the "goods," but my mate did not understand, see, taste, or smell the tricks that had been laid before us. As a result, we are no longer together. But what I learned the hard way will be with me the rest of my life. I am not ashamed or afraid to say that I should have chosen to seek after my Father first. Then loving unconditionally would have been easier.

Seek first the Kingdom of God. Be blessed in knowing a hard truth. Lust, when tainted by the enemy, will murder your self-esteem, ambitions, hope, faith, and relationships. But love, fostered by God, is life to your entire being, to all who meet you, to your relationships, and especially to your soul.

### *Testimony-Awaiting My King in Birmingham, Alabama*

The roller coaster sin ride that I was on was not worth it. Sex outside of marriage is a road to empty emotions. I wanted love so much that I settled for lust. I didn't have self-worth or know how to protect my temple. Today I understand that I am a holy treasure. I will continue to seed for my husband and never fill my temple with trash, but reserve its purity and wait for my real king to find me.

# Preparing for Marriage

You have received the mate God selected just for you. Marriage is honorable in the sight of the Lord. This section contains the keys to prepare you for your lifelong journey, as well as testimonies from couples about successful marriages.

# 6

# The Meaning of Symbols On Your Wedding Day

*Also, the man was not created for the woman. The woman was created for the man.* [10] *That's why a woman should have her head covered. It shows that she is under authority. She should also cover her head because of the angels.*

[11] *But here is how things are for those who belong to the Lord. The woman is not independent of the man. And the man is not independent of the woman.* [12] *The woman came from the man, and the man is born from the woman. But everything comes from God. (1 Corinthians 9-11)*

## The Veil

The wedding veil, symbolizing a wife's submission to her husband, had its inception in days of old when a bride stood beneath a canopy to signify she was under the protection of her groom. It was not white, as is the custom today, but was yellow in ancient Greece and red in ancient Rome. The veil originally symbolized the bride's virginity, innocence, and modesty.

## The Unity Candle

The unity candle is a large candle set up near the bride and groom. The bride and groom each hold a lit tapered candle and together light the larger candle. Then each blow out their individual candles, with the unity candle representing two becoming one.

## The Ring

The ring symbolizes eternity, endlessness, unbroken union and strength. Wedding rings are given as tokens of unending love for one other.

## The Wedding Dress

In Biblical times, most dresses were blue, symbolizing purity. In China and Japan, brides traditionally wore white. White is the color of mourning, which is thought to be appropriate, as the bride is leaving her family of birth to join her husband's, symbolizing death. In ancient Rome, white symbolized a joyful celebration. In the twentieth century, white stood for purity. Today it is a symbol of happiness.

## The Vow

The bride and groom make vows to God. Not keeping these vows means they are not honoring their promise to God.

# 7

# *Premarital Counseling*

## By Ministers Jerome and Rhonda Thomas

Premarital counseling is a vital part of the preparation for marriage. Counseling as a preventive measure that helps couples maintain a more lasting and successful relationship. Premarital counseling focuses on issues of past relationships as they relate to the current one. Most couples ignore unresolved issues from past relationships. Often it is the beginning of dealing with rejection, hurt, and disappointment, unresolved issues that can continue for years.

Both spouses have been shaped by positive and negative influences from childhood and adult encounters. Therefore, they have predetermined ideas of what their relationship should be. Without premarital counseling many marriages end in divorce. Counseling increases the chances for success.

Marriage is a covenant between two people and God. God created the sanctity of marriage for two people to live in harmony and in His purpose. If couples established their relationship on the principles of God's word and teachings, there would be more successful Christian marriages, a decrease in the divorce rate, and productive communities. Marriage is a lifetime. When a couple understands the vows, the level of commitment to their spouses and to God, they take their covenant more seriously.

Sometimes the pressure of planning and financial responsibilities becomes overwhelming and premarital counseling becomes secondary when it should be a priority. During the counseling process many issues that have gone unnoticed become visible. Romans 8:28-29 teaches that the goal of all believers is to become more like Christ. All that happens in a person's life is divinely orchestrated. (Divinely means "by God.") Therefore, if we rely on God's word to guide us, we can meet the right person and have a fulfilling life. The following should be emphasized during counseling:

- **Finances**
- **Premarital sex**
- **Love**
- **Commitment**
- **Trust**
- **Communication**
- **Respect**

Although this is only a partial list, it provides an overview of issues couples must address during courtship. Many are rarely discussed. One of the most difficult and important issues is unconditional love. Many marriages end in divorce because couples do not understand the concept of unconditional love and have preconceived notions of what they want their mate to be. If the relationship is ordained and predestined by God, partners will learn to embrace one another's faults, differences, and obstacles. God allows differences to bring balance in relationships. Scripture declares, *"Let the strong bear the infirmities of the weak."(Romans 15:1)*

If one mate is weak in one area, the other mate will usually have a greater strength in that area. God equips couples with balance and strength to love unconditionally. Instead of placing demands on one another, mates need to make the commitment to trust and love unconditionally. God loves all, regardless of our past failures or disappointments.

Another key to a successful marriage is effective communication. By spending time and communicating with each other during the courtship, couples can develop healthier relationships. Effective communication develops openness, honesty, and respect. Christian premarital counseling should address these issues so couples have an opportunity to correct their mistakes. When Christian counseling invites Jesus, it is considered a three-fold cord, according to Ephesians 4:12.

There is no perfect marriage. There will be problems, but believers have an obligation to correct them. God uses principles to illustrate natural concepts. Prior to laying the foundation of a new home, you must first grade the land. If the foundation is laid properly, it will be difficult to shake. Without Christian counseling, the foundation is unstable because problems are not recognized and addressed.

To have a marriage of purpose and success, couples must correctly apply the word of God. They must know, study, and practice it. When couples rely on the word of God as their source, their relationship thrives. When a husband and wife submit to the word, it is easy to submit to each other. God's word should always be the counseling authority of Christian living. Husband and wife must demonstrate the life that Christ exemplified according to His original plan. Marriage is not a life sentence; it is a sentence to life. Enjoy the journey.

# 8

# Preparing To Be
# A Husband Pleasing To God

## By Minister Kevin Lewis, Ph.D.

After contemplating the words of their spiritual treatise, many men endeavor to craft the words that will inspire a husband to please God. They try to understand, with a spiritual process, the character, mindset, spiritual heart, and favorable focus that pleases Jehovah. This is not an easy task, but it is possible to find clear direction from the Spirit of God, the word of God, the flow of His anointing, and inspired words from gifted men who have set their faces to seek the wisdom of God concerning the destiny of man. Many of you have undoubtedly had conversations concerning characteristics of good and bad husbands, husbands who have sought the heart of God and husbands who have played the role of the great pretender.

It is important to discuss the true nature of a man and principles that aid a husband in finding, within himself, focus, clarity of purpose, and a blueprint of success to find what God wants a man to become as a husband.

What is the true nature of a man? The answer to this question has been distorted throughout many generations. The original answer was penned by Moses when God said, *"Let Us make man in Our image."(Genesis 1:26)*. It goes on to express dominion to man to rule over the earth, birds, animals, and creatures of the sea.

What does it mean to be made in the image of God? When you look in the mirror, you find an image of yourself staring back. You do not see yourself staring, but an *image* of yourself. The mirror provides a clear reflection, just as God, who crafts all of us, has an image of Himself. He desires all of us not only to look like Him, but to reflect His character, take dominion over that which He gives us, act and respond the way He would, and represent Him in all matters on the earth.

In 1896, Charles Sheldon coined the phrase, "What Would Jesus do?" As creations of God's glory, our actions should be predicated on the will of God, utilizing His Son as a model, His Spirit as a guide, and His word as a blueprint.

It is a man's responsibility to follow after His Glory so that God might perpetuate His will for our lives. Realize that it is impossible to please God if we fail to operate in His will. Solomon reminded us in the Book of Proverbs 3:5 that our committed trust in God and acknowledgment of His wisdom will foster clear direction for the paths that we must follow as men. In Psalms 37: 3-5, Solomon's father, King David, taught that this trust, in God's way, leads to the ability for us to do well and prosper. He reminds us that our delight should always be in Him as He perpetuates the desires of our hearts.

David reminds us that this level of relationship comes with a sincere commitment to follow after the prudence, wisdom, and proverbial way of God in all aspects of our lives. If we follow these principles, the platform will be set to follow after God's will in all things.

There is something to be said about relationships between fathers and sons as we endeavor to understand the nature of being a man. Solomon learned from his father, David, the ways of God, the ways of praise that please God, and the humility in understanding that we are not God, only He is. God the Father's intention is that the relationships we have with our earthly fathers mirror the relationship we share with Him, our Heavenly Father. Some people may have relational issues with their earthly fathers or never have known them at all. Jehovah offers himself as a surrogate Father for every man, providing direction, purpose, clarity, protection, stability, affirmation, and love, so that all might have what they need to succeed in life.

At age five, I realized the absence of my earthly father in the home and adopted Jehovah as my Father and Jesus as my brother. God provided my every need, protected me, loved me in spite of myself, taught me how to be a man, and gave me clear direction about my purpose. And when He felt it was time, God returned my earthly father to me, allowing me to understand what it was like to have a loving father. He did not just return him to me as my earthly father; God reaffirmed our love, commitment, and friendship in the truest sense of the word.

As my father battled cancer, we shared truths concerning what it takes to be a man. At that time, my father knew his life was drawing to a close and wanted to share something special with his only son to carry me through the challenges of life.

My father taught me that there is more to being a man than just having a penis between your legs. We boast of having two heads. So many of our men today think with their head, not their brain. The result of using that brainless head are unplanned and unwanted pregnancies, bringing unwanted children into the world, neglected by their parents or families.

My father reminded me that the Bible characterizes the man as a leader, the priest of his household, the strength of his family and community. Too often, men do not see themselves in that light, and neither do their wives. The strength of our families rests with the truth of that wisdom. But in a decaying "real world," men lose focus, shack up, play out, and pretend to be more than they really are. They are often financially overextended, emotionally stressed, leaving a dismal future.

My father imparted the concept of responsibility, duty to family, and a shared love of God. We frequently had conversations from scripture about manhood. My father desperately wanted to share his wisdom as he neared death. I hear him every day reminding me that to be a man means never to quit, but stay the course, be responsible for those things God has given you dominion over, and live life *to please Him*.

Proverbs 18:22 talks about God's intent for man in marriage, *"He who finds a wife finds a good time, and obtains favor with (and from) God."* God is wise in crafting His direction for us in ways that we can comprehend, if we believe in Him. In the previous passage, Solomon says that favor is given to him who finds a wife.

You may remember times you cried and asked God to free you from your bondage. That is because you failed to realize what God had given you. The book of Matthew declares *that whenever two or three are gathered together in God's name, He's with you. (Matthew 18:20)*, and that *if two of you would simply agree by faith in prayer, God would give you what you ask.*

God is the creator of marriage and has set forth standards that must be followed to develop a successful marriage. Did you have sex with your wife before marriage? If your answer is yes, to whom did you give your honor? Was it God or Satan? It is Satan's desire that you honor him by committing premarital sex and denying the word of God and God's honor.

God desires that you prosper in all you do by the word. God has many blessings waiting for you if you follow His word. When we marry, He desires to favor us in all things, to bless us with His goodness and His mercy, as we walk in committed fellowship with Him. If you begin your relationship by honoring God and remaining faithful to Him in the relationship he gives you, you will please Him.

Remaining in God's favor requires that you stand in the faith of God, unwavering and undoubting. It is not easy to be the priest of your household, but that is why God gave you His armor, with instructions, "after having done all, Stand." The book of Ephesians, Chapter 6, reminds us that as we continue in this journey, we must stand for our mates, through the moments of confusion and pain, shielded by faith and standing rightly with God. Truth must follow you and your loins without temptation. You must continue on the path of peace and pray with and for your mate. Pray for her strength and faith. Pray that wisdom guides her through life's trials. Cover her with your love and protection. Pray that the angels of heaven protect her. Pray that God strengthens your marriage. Pray her through her changes in life. Pray for increased revelations in all things pertaining to your relationship. Pray through your pain, through the lack of communication, until God renders a breakthrough.

Some of you may think your wife is not worth it. Ask yourself, when you function in gross disobedience to God, lusting, doubting, failing to yield to His authority, non-responsive to His word, does God say that you are not worth it? Remember the Cross of Calvary and stand.

As you continue to live in an activated faith and to walk in a progressive commitment to the word of God, remember that when you are weak, God is strongest in your life. The Apostle Paul declared *"My God shall supply all your need according to His riches in Glory by Christ Jesus." (Philippians 4:19)* Whatever need you think you may have, God can supply it for you.

Jesus declared, *"If you abide in me, and my words of abide you, you can ask whatever you will, and it shall be done for you." (John 15:7)* The Apostle Paul reminds us, *"Now unto him that is able to do exceeding abundantly above all that we ask or think, according to the power that work it in us." (Ephesians 3:20)*

God yearns for your faithfulness that He might bless you with riches and glory. If you commit your ways unto the Lord and follow Him, if you commit your marriage to Him and to your wife in love unto Him, there is a blessed assurance that follows you, ***that you please God.***

Learning to be responsible is a process. As men, we cannot be trapped by conceit or pride. We must learn to make decisions and live with the moral conviction that fosters our positive leadership. Then we can overcome life's pitfalls and show our children what a strong man can do. So posture yourselves for this journey; it won't be easy. Plant a positive seed, an achievable goal, and a dream that can come true. Cultivate these with responsible thought and action, and watch the successes of life unfold.

# 9

# Preparing To Be
# A Wife Pleasing To God

Being single can be seen as preparation for marriage. When the single woman is fully submitted to God, He fulfills the role as husband, father, and brother. He is omnipresent. God's ultimate goal is to prepare his daughter to be ready to receive her husband. This is not a process that happens overnight; it takes time, patience, obedience, and willingness.

Here are keys to win the heart of God in becoming the wife pleasing to Him.

## Submission

*Wives, submit to your own husbands, as to the Lord. For the husband is head of the wife, as also Christ is head of the church; and He is the Savior of the body. Therefore, just as the church is subject to Christ, so let the wives be to their own husbands in everything. (Ephesians 5:22-24)*

Submission should not be difficult. When you were single, you submitted to God in everything. Your husband is the head of you; you must trust that the decisions he makes are from God. The marriage vows state to "love, honor, and obey."

This means through times of weakness or strength, richer or poorer, even when you want something and he says no. You are to be an understanding, submitting, loving, supportive wife and know that he has your best interest at heart. You must ask him before you do anything, even when you feel his behavior is inappropriate. Pray to the Lord about the situation. *Trust in the Lord with all your heart, and lean not on your own understanding; In all your ways acknowledge Him and He shall direct your paths. (Proverbs 3:5-6)*

When the inappropriate behaviors happen, you may feel like you do not want to cook, clean, or do the laundry. This is the flesh talking; you must force yourself to be what God created you to be, the helpmate to your husband. For example, one day my husband and I were arguing, and I was very upset.

The Lord spoke to my spirit and said "Cook him breakfast."

My first thought was, "Why should I?"

God said, "This is what I asked you to do."

So I made breakfast. I placed my husband's plate on the table and called him. He looked at it and walked away. God was testing me to see if I was going to be obedient and submit with love and gentleness, and I passed.

If you are confused about being the submitting wife, speak with wise counsel. It may be your First Lady or a mother of the church who has been married many years. It is not wise to speak to a single friend about your marriage situations because she would not understand.

Most Christian men take the role as head of the house seriously. If you feel he is being controlling or demanding, seek God and pray about it. Invite God to enter your relationship. Whatever words or instructions are revealed by the Holy Spirit, allow confirmation through the mouths of two or three witnesses. In marriage, both the husband and wife need to be clear as to their roles. As you submit to each other, with God being first, you will both feel confident in your roles. Ephesians 5:21 talks about submitting to one another in the fear of God. Trust God and your husband and your household will receive the blessings. This requires work by both of you.

## Love

In the book of Jude 1:12, agape is a Greek word that means love. We are to love with agape love, an unfailing love. This is the love that Christ has for all His children. No matter what we have done wrong, He loves us unconditionally. Even through the struggles and imperfections your husband may have, it is your duty to pray to the Lord and ask for deliverance and whatever you need to support him so he can conquer his struggles. Love is the greatest gift of all and covers a multitude of sin.

*Love suffers long and is kind; love does not envy; love does not parade itself, is not puffed up; does not behave rudely, does not seek its own, is not provoked, thinks no evil, does not rejoice in iniquity, but rejoices in truth; bears all things, believes all things, hopes all things, endures all things. Love never fails (1 Corinthians 13: 4-8.)*

It is important to express the love you have for your husband at all times. Do not hold back even when the marriage is challenging. The love that brought you together in the beginning will carry you to victory. Always speak with love; never speak death or evil words.

Following is a love quiz to help you identify the love you share with your husband by speaking love language.

## Love Language Quiz

Fill in the blanks with the 2-3 top things you love, like, admire, and feel about your husband.

1. I love when we

_____

_____

(3 things)

2. I love when you

_____

_____

(3 things)

3. I like when we

_____

(2 things)

4. I like when you

_____

_____

(3 things)

5. I feel so close when we

_____

(2 things)

6.  I feel so close when you

_____

_____

_____

(3 things)

7.  I know you are thinking of me when

_____

_____

(2 things)

8.  I admire you when

_____

_____

_____

(3 things)

9.  I feel so confident in being your wife when you

_____

_____

_____

(3 things)

## Prayer

Pray for your spouse more than you pray for yourself. Men are faced with many challenges daily, and it always great to have a wife who is willing to pray and even fast for him. *Commit your way to the Lord, Trust also in Him, and he shall bring it to pass. (Psalm 37:5)* Praying, be patient and wait on the Lord. God will grant it when He sees you being faithful; He will bless your family. Make time to pray with your spouse even through the difficult times. Satan loves division and distractions to keep you from coming together. Always invite God into your marriage in the area of prayer; He is the center holding both parties together.

## Trust

*"Casting all your care upon Him, for He cares you. (1 Peter 5:7)* This lesson teaches you to trust God with all decisions in your life. It is rewarding to show the same respect for your husband with every decision he makes for your

family. It is key to boost his confidence. Even when he makes poor decisions, ask God to give him clarity so you both can have a full understanding.

## *Growing In the Lord*

More women than men go to church. They seem eager to share Christian values with their spouses and families to help them grow spiritually, socially, and mentally. As you continue your walk with the Lord as the helpmate God called you to be, continue to read your word daily. *But seek first the kingdom of God and His righteousness and all these things shall be added to you. (Matthew 6:33)*

## *Communication*

*Let the words of my mouth and the meditation of my heart be acceptable in your sight, O' Lord, my strength and my Redeemer, (Psalm 19:14)*

Communication is important in your marriage. Speak with your Christian counselor about ways to communicate in a healthy way without screaming or name calling. Learn how to fight fairly. A counselor might advise you to go outside the home to a public place to discuss your concerns where it is difficult to raise your voice. Be respectful and allow your mate to finish his or her thought. Talk often to stay connected with each other. A healthy marriage takes a lifelong commitment of working together.

## *Developing Quality Time*

Take time to do what you both like, alternating between what you like and what he likes. If he is a sports fanatic, you could learn to like sports. If you enjoy the ballet or opera, he could learn to enjoy this with you. You are two people becoming one and sharing what you both love to do. Watch a movie or prepare a meal together; this is your time together.

## *Matters With Your Spouse*

It is best to keep personal matters between you and your husband. Obtain wise counsel. *A wise man will hear and increase learning and a man of understanding will attain wise counsel. (Proverbs 1:5)* Do not talk about problems in your marriage with others; seek Christ's counsel. Pray to God; He already knows about the problem, but He likes it when you tell him anyway.

## Forgiveness

*Hatred stirs up strife, but love covers all sins. (Proverbs 10:12), Do not rejoice when your enemy falls, and do not let your heart be glad when he stumbles. (Proverbs 24:17) If your enemy is hungry, give him bread to eat; and if he is thirsty, give him water to drink; for so you will heap coals of fire on his head, and the Lord will reward you. (Proverbs 25:21-22)*

When you forgive someone who has sinned against you, it releases any hurt, bitterness, or anger you have toward them. Bring into prayer to your father in Heaven so he can search your heart. *Create in me a clean heart, O God, and renew a steadfast spirit within me. (Psalm 51:10.)* Jesus says, *"And whenever you stand praying, forgive, if you have anything against anyone, so that your Father also who is in heaven may forgive you your trespasses." (Mark 11:25)*

Harboring non-forgiveness taints your prayer. When my husband and I were newlyweds, he did something to offend me, and I could not move past it. It took me almost a year to allow it to break from my spirit, but it impacted our marriage. I was able to share my feelings with him. He hadn't realized he had offended me. He said he was under pressure and didn't go about it with a Godly perspective.

Once I let go to allow God, I was able to forgive my husband and speak openly about the problem.

# 10

# Testimonies From Successful Marriages

These testimonies are meant to minister to your heart, spirit, and mind.

# A Special Testimony-
# Changing a Generation

## By Bishop Paul and Dr. Debra Morton, Atlanta, Georgia

After 30 years of marriage, we found the keys to a successful marriage: God, commitment, communication, and a lot of love. We have learned over many years that working together in every aspect of marriage is the main ingredient in a lasting and fruitful marriage. We are blessed to have three wonderful children and three grandchildren. As pastors serving God and His people, it is imperative that we are true examples of a Godly marriage. It is one thing to *say* we have a good marriage, but we practice what we preach. We are blessed to have each other.

## *Testimony- Key Ingredients in Atlanta, Georgia*

Having been married now for almost 20 years, I feel confident to say that to sustain in a marriage; you must have these three ingredients:

## *Faith*

It takes faith in God, even when you lose faith in yourself, your spouse, or marriage.

## *Obedience*

It takes obedience in what God has spoken to you, even when the instructions are difficult to obey.

## *Love*

Most of all, it takes love for your Father in heaven to continue to have *faith* sometimes in a faithless situation, to continue to be *obedient* to the Father even when it makes you uncomfortable, and to *love* even when a person or situation is not easy to love.

*Faith* in God, *obedience* in God's will, and a *love* for God are what has kept my marriage, my mind, and my family together. It is challenging at times, but God has been there through it all.

## *Testimony-Blessed in Harrisburg, Pennsylvania*

## *Values and Beliefs*

God is the Almighty One and parents are the number one role models. My parents recently celebrated their fiftieth wedding anniversary, and it was a special time for all five of their children. My mom stressed the importance of giving and devoted over twenty years of her life as a pianist and organ player for the church. I watched my parents' relationship evolve over the years because, no matter how tough things were, they believed that a family intact can go farther than a family divided. As the children left the nest to start their own families, my mom, who was always on the go, began staying home and spending more time with my father. My parents even moved from their small hometown to a major city to be near my oldest sister, who could help take care of them.

I learned the value of education and consistency from my dad. He worked at the same government job for 37 years and left for work every day by 6:30 A.M. He rarely missed work and worked a second job as a cook three nights a week. He had less than a tenth-grade education but made sure all five children went to college. That value is being passed down to all his grandchildren. His father left when he was eight years old and he never saw him again. He vowed he would never do that.

## Testimony-Servants of the Highest God in Decatur, Georgia

Marriage is made in heaven, but it is a lifelong ministry here on earth. My husband and I have been married for seven years and have truly worked through the portion of the wedding vows "for richer or poorer, in sickness and in health." We survived the rough times by entering this covenant in a spirit of holiness.

You must be holy and obedient to God's will to succeed. We are overcoming the odds, not only by the blood of the lamb and the word of our testimony, but by daily dying to self. We do as God instructs us to do, to esteem the other higher than ourselves. It is not easy.

When you sacrifice and purposefully elevate your spouse, you have promoted yourself because, through the marriage agreement, two become one. You have to agree to disagree, realizing that the final outcome rests on the word of God. Flesh, emotions, and opinions will rise, but obedience to God's manual (the Bible), not mankind, is the only way for your marriage to survive. Christian premarital counseling is also important.

## Testimony-Happily In Love in Atlanta, Georgia

So you want to be married? Are you going forward, standing still, or backwards?

This is my story of why I got married and stayed married against all odds. When my husband asked me to marry him, it took me by surprise because we were young and still in college. He said he was afraid that somebody else would take me away from him. I didn't understand love the way I do now, but that seemed like love to me. I agreed to marry him because I loved him as much as I could at that time in my life. He had all the qualities I wanted in a man. Thirty-five years later, we are more in love than when we got married.

Marriage validates Christian values; living together unmarried does not. When you decide to marry, you must consult with God. You must have a mutual respect for one another and trust your mate with your secrets and your heart. We have learned to meet each other halfway and give one hundred percent of ourselves. We love the way God wants us to love, unconditionally.

Treat your marriage like a covenant, not a contract. Contracts always have an out-clause, whereas covenants are for life. A man and woman get married when they are committed for life. You must decide that you can live with the other person's bad habits and love unconditionally.

Our son recently called from college and asked me how he would know when he was truly in love. I told him that when he wants her as much as he wants his next breath, he will know that he wants to spend the rest of his life with her. He has been happily married for four years now.

## *Testimony-41 Years Strong in Bloomfield, Connecticut*

## *A Happening Became Happier, A Sentiment More Sentimental, A Memory More Memorable*

The Lord blessed us with 41 years of marriage and two sons. We learned to place God first in our marriage. We faced ups and downs, but through prayer and faith in God, our marriage remains strong. In any marriage there are disagreements, misunderstandings, and arguments. But what has blessed our marriage is Christ working in our lives.

Communication is the key. You must know how to talk to one another, pray for one another, respect one another, and love one another. Keep the passion in your marriage. Be sensitive to each other's needs and desires, spend time together, and even date. Maintain a balanced relationship with your spouse and your children. Remember the vows you took, "to have and to hold each other in sickness and health, for richer or poorer, from this day forward until death do ye part." God honors marriage, and we must also.

## *Testimony-Words to the Women of God in Hartford, Connecticut*

Women often wonder how to keep their husbands interested in them. A woman needs to act and think like a lady at all times, even in public. She must know what makes her and her husband happy. Men do not require a lot. While dating, my wife I realized that I desired a woman who could hold her own but was not afraid to ask for help from her mate. She would be attentive and caring, but not to the point of suffocation. She would know when to be with her girlfriends and when to stay home. She would know when her man needed support and when he needed to do something without her help. She would know that being loud is not a substitute for being heard. She would know when to hold him and when to leave him alone. Some women give too much and the man gets spoiled. Some give too little and the man strays. If you can find that thin line of balance, things will be easier.

*Testimony-Childhood Sweethearts in Greenville, North Carolina*

Marriage is about compromising, listening, and sharing. I have been married to my childhood sweetheart for 17 years. We have had our challenges, but I have found that communication is the best way to keep marriage strong. You have to willing bend. My husband and I vowed to love, honor, and cherish each other "till death do us part," and we meant those words. Quitting is not an option for us, no matter how rough it gets. We know that the major key to a successful marriage is unconditional love.

# 11

# *Speaking Life or Death Into Your Marriage*

## By Yolanda Marshall

*"Death and life are in the power of the tongue." (Proverbs 18:21).*Each of us is held accountable, not only for what we do in life, but also for what we say. God has charged us to speak words that will edify each other; this is our responsibility as believers. *"Let no corrupt communication proceed out of your mouth, but that which is good to the use of edifying, that it may minister grace unto the hearers. And grieve not the Holy Spirit of God, whereby ye are sealed unto the day of redemption. Let all bitterness, and wrath, and anger, and clamour, and evil speaking, be put away from you, will all malice: And be ye kind one to another, tenderhearted, forgiving one another, even as God for Christ's sake hath forgiven you." (Ephesians 4:29-32)*

When you consider marriage, communicate with positive, encouraging, uplifting words.

### *Speaking Life Into Your Marriage*

Speaking life into your marriage brings joy. The joy of the Lord will give you strength and happiness in your marriage. A husband and wife thrive when they hear things like "Baby, I love you," "You are a beautiful woman," "You are a handsome man," "We can make it if we trust God and let Him lead our life," "You are such a blessing to me."

Such words will produce healthy fruit that every marriage needs to survive and be a Godly marriage.

Ladies, speak life into your marriage and be kind to your husband. You will see how your positive words will make a difference in your marriage and bring out the good from deep within your husband's soul. Encourage him, pray for him, build him up, and stand beside him as he seeks God's face for direction.

Men, you will see your wife's worth when you speak life into your marriage. Show how much you value her by speaking only positive words that will bless her spiritually, emotionally, and socially.

## Speaking Death Into Your Marriage

When a husband or wife speaks death into their marriage, they are basically cursing it with negative talk. Many marriages have dissolved because the husband, wife, or both have not been able to tame their tongues. Positive communication derives from positive thoughts. Negative communication derives from negative thoughts. Negative communication can be detrimental to a marriage, causing pain, hurt, confusion, doubt, and fear.

Being bitter, angry, or unforgiving will prevent a couple from speaking positive words that will bless their marriage. Instead, they will speak negative words that will curse their marriage. If a spouse says negative things like "I hate you," "You make me sick," "I don't know why I married you," or resorts to name calling, he or she needs to practice speaking words that will encourage, even when there are differences.

If you are speaking death into your relationship and are bitter, angry, or unforgiving before marriage, that will not change after you are married unless you receive "a touch from God." You can ask God to forgive you for not speaking life and to anoint your tongue and bless you to speak that which will glorify Him. Then you will find it easier to uplift each other prior to marriage. Remember that you can never do anything alone; both of you need God's guidance.

Never let the devil tell you it is okay to use condescending speech. If you do not have something good to say, do not say anything. When you approach the alter, you are becoming one in the sight of God, so be careful not to offend each other with your words.

# 12

## ℱinances

Statistics show that the number one reason for divorce is disagreements over money and how to manage it. This chapter focuses on your financial situation before marriage.

### Before You Say I Do!!

**By Pastor Hakeem J. Webb**

The first institution created by God was marriage, which gave way to family. The marriage institution was originally designed for husband and wife to be co-rulers over the earth and all His creation. However, since the fall of Adam (man), the devil has used strife and confusion to destroy the family because he knows he will never have a family to enjoy and wants the same for you.

One of the major areas in the family the devil attacks is finances. For example, if the wife spends money recklessly without the husband knowing, this lack of communication may result in an argument. This may escalate to the point that they are not speaking, resulting in a lack of sexual intimacy. During this time, the devil is certainly talking to them separately. The wife may think, "If he really loved you, he wouldn't be upset over that little bit of money you spent. After all, he bought something for himself last week."

The husband may think, "She spent money and she's not even going to have sex with you either? Doesn't she know a man has needs?" Now the husband is not only angry about the money; he is sexually frustrated and an open target for the enemy. He goes to work the next day and rides the elevator

56

with the pretty receptionist. She compliments him, he feels good, and before you know it, they are having dinner and ultimately sex.

*And Adam said, "This is now bone of my bones, and flesh of my flesh; she shall be called Woman, because she was taken out of Man. Therefore, shall a man leave his father and his mother, and shall cleave unto his wife; and they shall be one flesh.*

*(Genesis 2:23-24)*

When Genesis 2:23-24 states "they shall be one flesh," God is speaking of the total being as He sees beginning and end. The first thing that becomes one or your spirits. Your mind, will, intellect, and emotions continue to develop. The marriage covenant sanctioned by God brings the two bodies together as one after vows are exchanged. Once the marriage is consummated, emotions are connected. The soul, which is a work in progress, creates the money problems. You have two individuals from two different backgrounds. One person may have been taught by his/her parents to live on a budget. The other person may not know about a budget. Often couples do not discuss money issues before marriage.

A candid discussion of finances before marriage will avoid problems down the road.

Each person should get a copy of his or her credit report and share it with the other. If there is debt, discuss it. It is usually the result of frivolous spending and poor money management. Questions may arise such as will you keep your finances separate or help pay the other's debts. A secular adviser might suggest keeping finances separate, but a Christian counselor might say to combine them. If you are not able to agree before marriage, it might be best to postpone the wedding until serious debt problems are resolved. Some advisers may suggest pre-wedding planning, including a prenuptial agreement. You must be honest before marriage to develop trust.

For Christians, prenuptial agreements are not necessary. You will not see the use of them anywhere in the Bible. The Bible should be the final authority in your life. A prenuptial agreement opens the door for divorce because it perpetuates fear. Also, how do you justify that you love the other person when half your goods are out of the scope of the marriage?

It's wise to also discuss your views and beliefs about money and investing. Discuss the following; Are you a spender or a saver? Does investing in the stock market make you fearful or excited? Who will handle daily finances, such as balancing the check book and paying bills? If you have different attitudes and habits in managing money, how might you accommodate those differences?

You might consider having joint accounts for retirement and education, separate accounts for individual investments. The key is that you both know what the other is doing and each party has access in case of emergency. Discuss retirement age and other goals. If one is looking forward to retiring at age 55 and the other is expecting to work until age 70, this may cause conflict if not resolved. Also discuss whether you want to own a home or rent. Do you both want to have children? If you agree that you want children, what issues might be associated with raising children, e.g., allowance, private or public schooling, childcare? How should children's education be paid? What are your understandings about giving to the church or other charities?

Other issues involve estate planning, child support if appropriate, etc. The last thing you want are surprises after the wedding. One of the criteria for a Christian to be married is premarital counseling with a pastor, minister, or priest. Couples should also consider talking with a Christian financial advisor, either through your church or an independent counselor. As believers you can go to Father God in prayer for help and direction; no situation is too difficult for Him.

Know that love is patient and will remove all burdens and destroy every yoke. Take your bills and together pray the prayer of agreement over your family, your finances, and your children. Speak the promises of God over them and no longer speak of defeat. Then watch and see how God, Jesus, and the Holy Spirit will get involved with your situation. Your finances will be resurrected. Remember, the devil's job is to keep you at odds, so don't let him win. The power of agreement is stronger than anything he could ever throw your way.

*Financial Tips*

**By Financial Advisor Zenobia Mims**

# GETTING YOUR FINANCIAL HOUSE IN ORDER

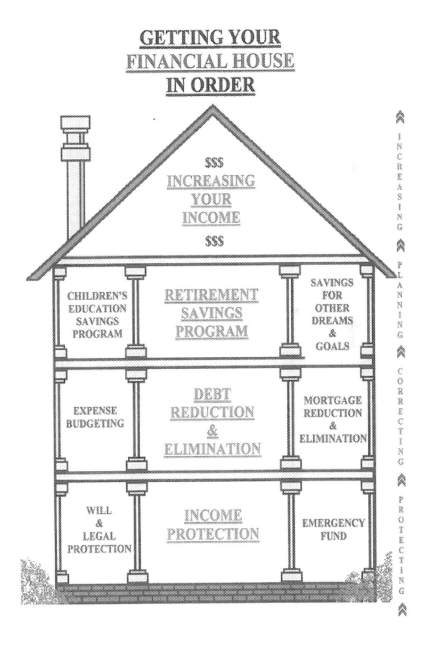

Couples need to discuss retirement, alternate sources of income, ways to reduce taxes, and investment potential, savings, and diversity of investment.

*Where Do You Begin?*

Christians often do not handle money as the Bible guides them, making poor financial decisions. *"My people are destroyed for lack of Knowledge".* *(Hosea 4:6)*

It is important to seek a financial advisor who can teach you on how to save money and become debt free. Begin by giving ten percent of your income to the Lord our God, saving the second ten percent, and handling faithfully the remaining eighty percent. It may take time to develop these habits. Consider earning additional income, adjusting your priorities (wants verses needs,) avoiding the credit card trap, investing in high-bearing accounts instead of savings accounts, and protecting your family with term life insurance, etc.

Establish three accounts: emergency fund, short-term savings, and long-term savings. Use the calculation below to determine how much you have earned since you started working and how much you have saved. Prior to marriage, talk about how you will handle these joint accounts.

A) **Average annual income (estimated):** _____

B) **Times number of years worked:** _____

C) **Equals total amount earned:** _____

D) **Amount of personal savings:** _____

E) **Divide D by C: =** _____% **of income saved**

Knowing the difference between a want and a need is critical. A need is a necessity of life – food, clothing, or shelter. A want is anything more than a need – the latest fashion, a new car, etc. Using a budget and knowing where your money goes each month will help you keep track.

## How to Manage Your Credit

**By Lady M**

Below are questions to assist in financial planning:
- How much is too much debt?
- How many credit cards are considered too many?
- How can you improve your credit score?
- What is the highest and lowest score?
- How can I keep from going into more debt?

### How much is too much debt?

Debt ratio explains how your monthly debt payments compare to your monthly income. A high debt ratio indicates that your monthly expenses are becoming unmanageable. It also might discourage lenders from loaning you money. Seek a credit counselor to assist you.

### How many credit cards are too many?

Three or more credit cards is a sign to lenders that you have the potential to get into too much debt too quickly. It may also cause banks to decline your applications for loans. Even if you don't have a balance on the cards you own, your bank knows you could run up charges quickly. Try to have no more than two credit cards.

### What is the highest and lowest credit score?

A poor credit score is between 580 and 619; a good score is 720 or higher. Work together; discuss the A-plus credit rating with a counselor regarding what you would like to have so you can focus on your investments.

### How can you improve your credit score?

Pay down your credit cards, keeping your balance below 30% of the credit limit for each card. If possible, pay your bills in full each month. Having a credit card for a long time shows a strong relationship with the lender. Check your credit report periodically. If you dispute anything, write a letter to all three credit bureaus (Equifax, Experian, and Transunion). State any errors, discrepancies or if there is an account that is not yours. Remaining a loyal customer, will help later if you need the company to forgive a charge or late payment or work out a payment plan.

### *How can I maintain debt without going into additional debt?*

The simple way to avoid more debt is to say no. When you receive pre-approval letters for credit cards in the mail or a store offers a discount on purchases if you apply for a credit card, say no. Look for coupons to save money.

# Conclusion

Marriage is a covenant between a man, a woman, and God. It is not to be taken lightly. If you are diligent in your devotion to God and know that your perfect mate will appear when you are ready, and according to God's plan, you will find him or her.

Have faith, love and honor God and one another, be the man or woman God wants you to be, asking Him for guidance, knowing that you are worthy and loving of all the best in your life, and He will bring you your perfect mate.

It will not happen overnight, so be patient. You are worth it!

## Tips For Planning Your Wedding Day

1. Pray together and ask the Lord to bless your engagement and union.
2. Pray about where you will begin your premarital counseling_ at church, Christian counselor, or group sessions.
3. Pray together about your budget.
4. Pray together about the type of wedding you will have.
5. Pray together about seeking a wedding planner to assist you.
6. Pray together about your honeymoon destination. If you are on a budget. Be creative and go somewhere affordable within driving distance.
7. Pray together on selecting your wedding ring.
8. Pray together about your guest list.
9. Make your planning as stress free as possible and enjoy your engagement and each other.

# Credits

Kelly Is Nice Photography (www.kellyisnice.com)
Photos inside of the book provided by Kelly Is Nice

Tia Greene Marketing & PR Agency www.tiagreenemarketing.com

Picture Lady Pinkie www.pictureladypinkie.com
Profile photo of Lady M provided by Lady Pinkie

Debbie Ellison Editorial Service